Le Corbusier's Hands

Le Corbusier's Hands

André Wogenscky
translated by Martina Millà Bernad

The MIT Press
Cambridge, Massachusetts
London, England

MIT Press books may be purchased at special quantity discounts for business or sales
promotional use. For information, please email special_sales@mitpress.mit.edu or
write to Special Sales Department, The MIT Press, 55 Hayward Street, Cambridge, MA
02142.

This book was set in Berthold Akzidenz Grotesk by MIT Press and was printed and
bound in the United States of America.

Library of Congress Cataloging-in-Publication Data

Wogenscky, André, 1916–2004
[Mains de Le Corbusier. English]
Le Corbusier's hands / André Wogenscky ; translated by Martina Millà Bernad.
    p. cm
Includes bibliographical references.
ISBN 0-262-23244-8
1. Le Corbusier, 1887–1965—Anecdotes. 2. Architects—France—Anecdotes. 3. Le
Corbusier, 1887–1965—Friends and associates—Anecdotes. I. Title.

NA1053.J4W6413 2006
720´.92—dc22   2005052050

10 9 8 7 6 5 4 3 2 1

Contents

Height

At the end of 1936 a young architecture student stepped into a building on 35 rue de Sèvres in Paris. He walked down the great hall of the ground floor. He went up the small, dark, dilapidated staircase, and shyly he stopped at the door of Le Corbusier's studio.

He almost turned around to leave without daring to open that door. He did not know that his entire life was going to heavily depend on that decision. He opened the door. He went in.

A stern-looking secretary came up to him. He asked if it would be possible to meet with Le Corbusier for a few moments, some time. She said, "It's difficult. He's very busy. I'll go see." She left and did not come back. Le Corbusier himself came.

It was then that he saw Le Corbusier.

A strange memory has remained with him of that first vision. He was very surprised that Le Corbusier wasn't taller than he was. He had read *Towards a New Architecture*; he was so enthused by his ideas and his projects, he expected to meet such a great man that he would not have been surprised if Le Corbusier had been five or six meters tall. And yet, there he was, so simple, and no taller than that shy, puny student.

Immediately, Le Corbusier met with him for an hour and a half, asked him all kinds of questions and, much less intimidating than his secretary, talked to him with warmth and simplicity. That same evening, after dinner, the young student started working at the studio as a draftsman. He did not know that he was going to work with Le Corbusier for twenty years, and to know him closely for thirty years.

His Hand

That same day, when Le Corbusier greeted him and extended his hand to him, the shy student put his hand in Le Corbusier's hand: his hand all wrapped inside a big hand.

Can hands remember?

Writing this text today, he still keeps in his hand the memory of the hand he shook.

His Step

A memory of a sound: the steps on the floor as Le Corbusier walked down the long hall at 35 rue de Sèvres, that same hall where, the evening of 1 September 1965, his body rested for a few hours under the blue, white, and red colors of the flag, in front of one of his black, white, and red tapestries. It was the same hall that Le Corbusier walked every day for half a century with his calm and regular step to do his architectural work.

That slow, regular step was the very rhythm of his personality. A rhythm drawn in space by the structure of his rigorous, slow, calm, regular, and exact buildings. It was the rhythm into which he introduced poetry.

Steps that seemed slow but that quickly went forward.

His Personality

The rhythm of his steps was the cadence of his personality: precise, uncompromising, but contradictory. Perhaps it belongs to men of genius to reconcile what is irreconcilable in themselves as well as in their work. Le Corbusier's character was the meeting of opposites. He was hard, even violent sometimes, in a state of inner rage that he tried to control, and yet gentle and even tender. He was gentle because he was strong. He was proud but modest, often self-doubting. He once even called his close collaborator and told him, "Am I not making a mistake? Will the inhabitants of the *Unité d'Habitation* at Marseilles be happy? Would you like to live in the Radiant City?" And it was left to that assistant, so tiny in comparison to him, to lift up his spirits.

He said several times that in the morning he woke up in the body of an idiot that disappointed him, but that by evening, after being in contact with others, he felt less stupid than them.

Calm and nervous, authoritarian and shy, battling and peaceful, intransigent and understanding, hard and gentle, active and contemplative, self-centered and generous, proud and modest, Cartesian and mystical, solid and emotional, clear-sighted and naive, engaged, yet free and alone.

His Hands

When we were with him, when we listened to him, we looked at his face. We waited for his smile; we wanted him to be happy. We tried to extract some meaning from the expression on his face. We looked at his mouth, a mouth whose lines often remained bitter, a bit disappointed. Sometimes his face froze up to protect his inner life: a grave and pensive face. He would go far away.

Then I would let my eyes go from his face down to his hands. I would then discover Le Corbusier. It was his hands that revealed him. It was as if his hands betrayed him. They spoke all his feelings, all the vibrations of his inner life that his face tried to conceal.

Two big, strong hands, very big, incised as if with a burin with very deep furrows. Muscled phalanxes. Vibrant, animated hands. Enveloping hands.

Hands that one might have thought Le Corbusier had drawn himself, with that trait made of a thousand small successive traces that seemed to look for one another but that in the end formed a precise and exact line, that unique contour that outlined the shape and defined it in space. Hands that seemed to hesitate but from which precision came. Hands that always sought, just like he did in his thinking, and on his hands one could read his anxiety, his disappointments, his emotions and his hopes.

Hands that had drawn, and were to draw, all his work.

Touching

The hand that loved touching, and taking.

He picked up pebbles and felt them in his hand to perceive their shapes. On his small desk in the studio he had a big marrowbone. He often took it; he looked at it with his fingers; he showed it. He showed the ossified fibers that ran crosswise through the interior of the bone. He talked about structure. For him it was not enough to see it. He felt it with his fingers.

He held the chisel, the pencil and the brush in his hand. The tool was not independent of the hand. It prolonged the touch. It made it possible to touch what was engraved, what was drawn or painted, even what was written.

> The tools in the hand
> The caress of the hand
> The life that we taste through
> The kneading of the hands.
> The view that we have when we touch.[1]

Taking

The hand that took, and held tight.

Marta and I had a German shepherd named Puck. On one of the days when Le Corbusier came to see us at Saint-Rémy-les-Chevreuse, he caressed the dog. Then he put his hand on the dog's nape and held Puck by the neck. He held it tighter and tighter. Puck started to growl. "Corbu, why are you holding him so tight? He's going to bite you." And Corbu replied: "I love to feel how far I can go."

Very often, in the confrontations that constitute human relations, Le Corbusier wanted to see how far he could go. And sometimes he "held" a bit too tight.

Body

The hand that held tight to know and to take. The hand was a source of knowledge and existence. He loved the body of things and the life of the bodies he perceived, not only through his eyes, but also through the hand that touched. He loved women's bodies. He often drew them and painted them, a little swollen because life, from inside, swells up the shapes that it inhabits. For him, woman was the indispensable complement, the form that allowed him to complete and unify his own form.

"On their side, from top to bottom, men have a perpetual tear. They are but half; they only feed life halfway. And the second half comes to them and binds itself to them."[2]

All thinking is tied to the body, to its volumes and shapes. Body and thought are not independent of each other. Form, by sight and by touch, enriches thought, and that thought, to manifest itself, must be shaped by the hand.

Effort

The hand that closed up and gripped to hold something and not let go. The hand that contracted in front of an obstacle, and the thought that tightened up when faced with an effort.

"There is nothing for those who do not strain their thoughts without suffering, each hour of the day, to know whether the hours that go by are good hours."[3]

All of Le Corbusier's life was about effort, tenacity, perseverance, will. He already knew that by age twenty-one:

"To tell you that my life is no joke, but intensive, necessary work, is pointless since, to go from being an engraver to becoming an architect of the idea that I've formed of this vocation, one must take a giant step.... But now that I know where I'm going, I could make the effort—full of joy and victorious enthusiasm—to take that step."[4] And still: "When the force that is in me tells me—prompted by an internal event—you can."[5]

To produce is to make an effort and sustain that effort. While in Punjab, on 6 November 1951, he wrote to his team at rue de Sèvres:

"Here everything is interesting, but it's all like a young child or a young elephant: it's relatively easy to get it started. Still we had to find the woman or Mrs. Elephant. But to get it out of the belly, we have to push very hard!!!"[6]

Perhaps one day he read the following statement by Seneca: "It is not because things are difficult that we do not dare, it is because we don't dare that they are difficult."[7]

Bitterness

Yes, there was often bitterness on Le Corbusier's face. His mouth tightened slightly. He seemed to look far away. His face closed up. His thoughts retreated from whoever was around him.

One is surprised to find that someone destined for such great things could harbor any bitterness. It was perhaps caused by disappointments in the hidden part of his life. Surely there were many disappointments in his work, a lot of opposition, many criticisms, much malice and meanness encountered, a great deal of bad faith against him. There were many failures in his hopes to build and put his ideas to work, and, yet, what a great success: an international renown quickly acquired, a considerable influence over all contemporary architecture and town planning, a crowd of admirers, many warm demonstrations of appreciation, numerous friends, a whole circle of young men committed to working for him, and the trust put in him by so many women and men.

Why, then, that bitter taste on his frozen lips, in his saddened eyes? Perhaps it is simply that geniuses are demanding beyond their achievements and that their demands exist within the realm of what cannot be achieved. Perhaps it is the strength to always want to do better, and the disappointment that one cannot produce better things. There was also in him the painter who would like to get ahead of the architect. Only incidentally, almost by chance, by force of circumstances, did he consider himself an architect.

"When I was thirteen and a half, I was made an apprentice in the engraving of watchcases: using copperplate engraving we decorated the back of big, round watches that men kept in their pockets. A contract tied me for four years. At the end of the third year, one of my teachers (a remarkable teacher) dragged me slowly away from that mediocre activity. He wanted to make an architect of me. I despised architecture and architects. That teacher, L'Eplattenier, initiated me to 1900 art movements, an eminent effusion of creative forces: nature, forms and reappearance of a style (a way of thinking).

At one of these turns was painting!!!

'No, never,' told me L'Eplattenier! 'You don't have any aptitude for painting!' (He was a painter himself). I was sixteen years old, I accepted the verdict and obeyed; I became involved in architecture."[8]

He saw himself first as a painter. He would have liked to be considered a better painter than architect. All his life he carried that duality and that disappointment at the core of his inner life. All his life he sometimes felt saddened by this.

But he was one. "The two parallel beings are like the two extremities of one single stick."[9]

What characterized him as well was the strength he had to overcome that bitterness, and the battle he won every day against it. Then his face would come back to life. His mouth smiled again. His eyes regained their brightness. His hand went back to drawing.

He drew river meanders.

Meanders

He looked at them from the airplane. He filled page after page with their sketches. The river meandered over the flat terrain. It slowly moved forward, creating curves, and those curves got rounder until they became circles. Upstream, alluvia deposited themselves while downstream from the curve the water ate slowly into the bank. Later, after centuries had gone by, the curves would meet again, a direct passage would be hollowed out, and the river would abandon the meander and flow in a straight line.

"River meanders mean that the course is perhaps sometimes very long, very rough, very unreasonable. It's the meander of complications and complexities."[10]

Complications, complexities, failures, disappointments: yes, very frequently. But also tenacity, perseverance: he seemed to have decided once and for all that he would never get discouraged. Through his attitude regarding life, he allowed me to understand that it is necessary to have the courage to refuse to get discouraged, and that it is only with many disappointments that some satisfactions are built.

The meander is the very image of his life, made of unrelenting effort, going around the obstacle, but without renouncing, eating into things, always eating into things so as to go deeper and find the passage through. Then, leaving behind the meanders, the disappointments, all bitter feelings and malicious events, going through it all and finding life again, perpetual birth, joy.

Like woman and like man, the river is made of what it receives: its sources, its tributaries, and its run-offs. It is with them that it creates its shape, and then it takes them to the sea.

La mer est redescendue
au bas de la marée pour
pouvoir remonter à l'heure.
Un temps neuf s'est ouvert
une étape un delai un relai

Alors ne serons-nous pas
Demeurés assis à côté de nos vies.

The Sea

After getting all contracted in front of the obstacle or failure, the hand led by thought and by will opened up and started all over again.

Like the sea.

"The sea has come down again at low tide to be able to go up again in time. A new time has opened up, a phase, a given period, a relay.

Then we won't remain seated by the side of our lives."[11]

Frankness

The hand that opened up again was the image of frankness, of honesty. Here I am, take me as I am. It was a hand that could not cheat nor lie.

"Lies are intolerable. When we live with lies, we die."[12]

He hated architectural lies. For fear of lying, he refused to design the chapel at Ronchamp.

The Dominican monks asked him to be the architect of a chapel to be built on top of a hill, the last hill to the south of the Vosges region, at Ronchamp, where for centuries there had been places of worship and where there used to be a pilgrimage chapel, which was destroyed during the last war. Le Corbusier refused. He had never built a church or a monastery, or any religious building of any sort. Le Corbusier refused because he was not a Catholic, because he was born in a Protestant family in Switzerland. His mother practiced and he himself received a Protestant education, but he was an agnostic. He said he did not know whether God existed or not and that without knowing, it was more honest to say "I don't know."

Le Corbusier replied, "No, I don't have the right to build a church, a Catholic chapel; I'm not a Catholic; you need to hire a Catholic architect." One day, he asked me to go to his home. He told me, "Father Couturier is coming to lunch and we have to talk about this chapel he wants me to build and that I don't want to build. Come then, Wogenscky, and join us, you are going to be at the lunch."

That day I was present at an extraordinary conversation. I can't think back about it without emotion. Me, I said nothing. I was sitting at the head of the marble table. On the right, Father Couturier was clad in his magnificent white frock. On the left, Le Corbusier, against the wall, defended his point of view. "I don't have the right! Hire a Catholic architect," and Father Couturier explained to him that the decision to ask Le Corbusier had been made on purpose, knowing full well that he was not religious. Finally he told him, "But Le Corbusier, I couldn't care less about your not being a Catholic. We need a great artist, and the aesthetic intensity, the beauty that you are going to make those who will come to the chapel experience, will allow those who have faith to find once more that which they come to seek. Art and spirituality will converge, and you would reach our goal much better than if we asked a Catholic architect: he would think he must produce a copy of an old church."[13] That left Le Corbusier thinking for a few seconds, and then he said, "Then I accept." And he designed the chapel at Ronchamp.

Building Oneself

One day somebody asked him: "Do you have a special trick, a method? How do you manage to do all you do?" He simply replied, "It's because my mother once told me: whatever you do, do it well."

Another day, while we were on a trip, we were looking at a street cleaner we had run into by chance. Le Corbusier told me, "You see, Wogenscky, what this man does is as important as what I do." Astonished, I asked him to explain. He explained it to me: the consequence of the act is the quality of what has been done. What we decide to do, our profession for instance, is less important than the value of the result and what we demand from ourselves in what we do. To try to do things well leads one to build oneself, tirelessly, like when we build a house. The quality of the result follows from this building of oneself.

It is one of the most powerful examples that I received from Le Corbusier: that kind of demanding struggle with oneself, a self that is never finished; as long as we are alive we build it, we polish it. It is something that evolves with each day as we build it. I can't remember who it was who said, "To turn one's life into a work of art." Le Corbusier could have said "To turn one's life into architecture."

That leads also to extreme honesty.

"Cubs and puppies show their natural inclinations; but men throw themselves immediately into acquired habits, opinions, and laws and either change themselves or easily disguise themselves."[14]

Le Corbusier did not disguise himself. His strength came from his having got rid of rules, established ways of doing or seeing, and routines. It is perhaps the strength of the self-taught. No school where one gets into bad habits. No "we do it like this." His school was the spectacle of life. It was free from all the rules, habits, and models that school and society put into our eyes. He was untouched by those conditioned reflexes that enslave so many architects. He started from zero in life and found in himself great cosmic, earthly, and human forces, energy fields that affected the body and the mind.

Open Hand

One of Le Corbusier's strengths was to know how to receive and to take. He looked, he touched, he noticed. He wanted to take and make his own. He took off with his backpack, went across Europe and around the Mediterranean. From his youth to the end of his life he filled numerous sketchbooks with drawings, observations, and ideas he wanted to keep. He stored up all he could. He yearned to see, to know, and to assimilate.

"I have received handfuls." [15]

"But when, in which one of our lives, do we finally become beings that open themselves up to receive?" [16]

The hand was open to receive. He had undoubtedly understood in his youth that it was necessary to be someone who never ceases to receive in order to become perhaps, and only very rarely, someone capable of offering.

"Open to receive, open also to let anyone come and take from it." [17]

"It is man who gives and man who receives. It is a mortal hand that offers it to us and a mortal hand that accepts." [18]

His whole life was a big open hand. At times he closed it up around the secret of his own being. And was there not as well in the *Open Hand* he designed for Chandigarh a secret, a call, a cry towards what cannot be grasped, a cry that nobody hears?

"Do not think that I am sending a request, Angel, and even if I did, you would not come. For my invocation is always full of refusal. Against such a strong current, you cannot go. My call resembles a tightened arm, and its hand, which opens itself up and reaches high to grab, remains open in front of you, as a defense and a warning. O you, Ungraspable, wide open." [19]

Picasso

Le Corbusier was intense. From his accumulated richness, assimilated and thought through, stemmed an energy field that emanated from him.

Along with some of his other collaborators, I was very fortunate to live an unforgettable day. Picasso came to spend a day at the construction site of the *Unité d'Habitation* at Marseilles. Le Corbusier had come down from Paris to welcome him. Walking around the site and eating lunch with them at the workers' canteen, all day we listened to those two men talk to each other. They cared a great deal about each other and shared a great friendship. Picasso was one of the very few contemporaries of Le Corbusier that the latter truly cared about. I think I remember how one day he told me that Picasso was a greater painter than himself.

All day long they outdid one another in a show of modesty. Each one tried to place himself lower than the other. It was marvelous. And what has left an indelible trace in my memory is the energy that emanated from each of them. We were inside a double energy field. Their voices were calm, their silences full of meaning. Their eyes were bright and their hands talked.

Candidness

He was candid. He often said, "I am naive." And he was often right about that. He presented himself as he was: innocent, trusting.

Several times during his life he trusted people who did not deserve his trust, and they deceived him.

He was essentially apolitical, but he put his trust on those whom he called the "councillors," those who had power. He went to them, and sometimes he naively made serious mistakes that would then leave him dismayed.

He was a very bad diplomat. When I went with him to decisive meetings, I was afraid. Sometimes his major obstacle was himself.

At La Rochelle he made his project fall through. For that city's extension, his urban plan envisioned a neighborhood of the Radiant City type comprising ten *Unités d'Habitation* on a vacant plot of land between La Rochelle and La Pallice. Soltan and I, during numerous trips and multiple meetings, prepared the ground as best we could. We were very happy because the Mayor seemed to be in agreement. He told us that he was ready to write to the Minister to express his desire that the project be built. But the Mayor had not yet met Le Corbusier. He wanted to see him. He asked that Le Corbusier come in person to present his project to the town council. We came back with Le Corbusier, who explained the project at a formal session. He praised the living conditions in the *Unités.* Then he added, "This housing will be as beautiful as that of ancient Mesopotamia." Frozen silence. The Mayor turned pale. Soltan and I did, too. The Mayor whispered in my ear, "He thinks we are a bunch of savages!" And everything foundered, *Unités d'Habitation* and Radiant City. That was in 1946, before the decision to build an *Unité* in Marseilles.

Almost the same story for the Meaux project: a Radiant City neighborhood with five *Unités d'Habitation.* We were on the site with the Mayor and Le Corbusier. Two magnificent hares ran off at galloping speed. The Mayor told us that it was always the female hare that went ahead of the male. Le Corbusier and I did not know that. Silence. Then Le Corbusier jokingly added, "Why not build little one-family houses on this site?" The Mayor did not like the joke. The Ministry's representative, who had been against the project all along, appreciated it even less, and another architect got the job.

Luckily, there were other times when Le Corbusier won over his clients.

Alone and In Silence

He was alone. No matter how close a friendship he had with anyone, even during the course of a conversation, or at a work meeting, sometimes Le Corbusier seemed to leave. He would retreat into his inner life, more populated than the world of men.

His real work was always solitary. Social life has a tendency to cut us up and to disperse us into small fragments. It is necessary to gather oneself up again, to get close to oneself, and for that, one needs to be alone.

"It is when one is alone that one fights against one's self."[20]

He protected his work.

One day he had asked me to go see him in his apartment. He wanted to talk to me in private. We were in his painting studio. The big revolving door started to open and in came his wife Yvonne. He sent her back ruthlessly. "You have no right to come here." I was shocked. I thought he was exaggerating, and yet I knew how much he liked her.

He did not like being with too many people. He hated meetings, and when in a group he remained silent. Sometimes somebody else had to speak for him. He was very protective of himself, and he was also mistrustful. Perhaps he knew the African saying, "Men don't have manes or tails, but to get hold of them they have the words coming from their mouths."[21]

Solitude is not selfishness. It is, on the contrary, expansion of oneself. It is not impoverishing.

"It is a great privilege to place oneself freely in front of one's self to let the inner forces rush forth."[22]

Joy

He loved to be happy. He enjoyed life's pleasures. He loved wine and *pastis.* He loved joking. His jokes and the jokes he liked were never tasteless. They came from the people and the street. He detested vulgarity. Occasionally somebody cracked a tasteless joke around him. He would not say anything, but the expression on his face became distant and his hands said he had not liked it. If his tastes were those of common folk, an aristocrat could also be discovered in him, perhaps without his even knowing it.

His bedside author was Rabelais. I told him I preferred Montaigne. He told me he preferred Rabelais. His reply makes me suspect he had not read much Montaigne, and, yet, there are similarities between him and Montaigne. I was never able to tell whether he read much or not. Maybe he did not. His immense general knowledge was not bookish. It had been acquired from lived experience. It came from his drawings, from his travels, from what he had seen and experienced. It was manual rather than intellectual.

He never burst out laughing, but one could very well tell when he was happy. His face and his hands said it and we would then feel something warm coming from him.

Intuitive and Calm

The life of his hands was also the image of his intuition.

On a given site, he could be seen feeling the earthly and cosmic forces going through it. Like animals do, he felt the lines of force, their intersections, the intense spots and the inert spots. His hand drew them in his sketchbook.

He felt the course of the sun and drew the rhythm of the day and of the night.

There was the intuition of the life of human beings on earth. He kept his distance from them, but he was close to them, as he observed and listened to them, drew them and understood them. He was clear-sighted.

He was not good at analyzing. He often did not know how to explain clearly what he was suggesting. He created in a receptive audience a kind of aesthetic and poetic resonance of his personal vision. He made one feel it rather than understand it rationally. In a meeting it was sometimes necessary to explain things for him. Wrapped up in his solitude and inside himself, he saw the problems and the solutions.

Out of a thousand pieces of information, out of a thousand scattered factors, he created a single thing. He integrated them. Each one of them became an element of a shape, depending on the others and acting on them. He saw in the same way that a composer hears.

Then, his hand would draw. Then, beyond all restlessness, he would be calm. His calmness did not destroy his desire or his passion. On the contrary, it concentrated them in their potential.

Work

First, he was a manual worker. He learned to engrave and chase watchcases. The trace of manual work remained in all his works: forms felt and shaped by the hand. He traveled around the Mediterranean. He liked all that architecture made with the hands according to human scale, in Greece, Turkey, the Mzab. That sculptural architecture erected with both hands was present in all his works, and could later be found at Ronchamp.

His hand was always drawing. He drew trees, leaves, and buds. To draw them was to have his fingers feel the seed that had made them. Their shape was not a random thing. It was organic, a life form. He drew landscapes, shaped by the forces of wind and water, by life, and by the human hand.

"The hand that contains so many inner lines and so many meanings around its perimeter, in its texture; it contains the character of the person, which means that the most hidden, most secret, most subjective, most elusive things can very well be revealed by a precise trait, a line on the hand, by the hand's muscles, by the shape of the hand."[23]

It was the head that guided the hand, but sometimes the hand guided the head.

He said, "I let it all go from my hand into my head." And, "Sometimes, it is my hand that precedes my mind."[24]

The head thought. The hand touched. The body sensed.

His hands acted up "head and hand combined, wherefrom stems in a quiet way the flesh and spirit of human work."[25]

While the head thought, it was best not to let the hand draw too early or too fast. Le Corbusier at work meant to wait first, and sometimes for a long time. I often worried about this. We would have to turn in a project on a given deadline, and Le Corbusier would wait. Sometimes it seemed that he had forgotten. He did not talk about it. He let it be born.

"When I am given a project, I am in the habit of putting it into my memory bank, that is to say, of not allowing any sketch to be made for months. The human mind is made in such a way that it enjoys having a certain independence: it's like a box into which one can throw in a haphazard way the elements of a problem. We then allow them to float, to stew and ferment. Then it comes a day when a spontaneous initiative from the inner self triggers it all: we take a pencil, a charcoal crayon, color pencils (color is the key to this process), and we give birth on paper. The idea comes out, the baby comes out. It has arrived in the world and it is born."[26]

He saw from the beginning just as the composer hears from the beginning.

"Not to draw, but to see first the project in one's head. The drawing is only useful to help with the synthesis of the thought-through ideas."[27]

"It is impossible to organize the pieces if you do not have the shape of the whole inside your head."[28]

Then, one day, he would come to the office at rue de Sèvres with a bundle of sketches, generally made on typing paper, with black pencil, ball-point pen, and mainly color pencils. It would all be there;

the entire project would be contained in them. At first we would have a hard time understanding these sketches. Then we would learn to read them, to see them. They contained the seed of the whole project. All we would have to do then was to tidy them up with a T-square and set square, and Le Corbusier would continue to see over the drawings in detail to the end. He would remain seated for a long time at our drawing boards. He clarified. He corrected. He reinforced the exactness and the rigor. He finished up. He made us draw certain details full-scale on a big blackboard that went all the way to the ceiling. The *loggia* of the *Unité* at Marseilles was drawn full-scale in this way and scrupulously put together. To the smallest detail, even at the building site, Le Corbusier drew and wanted to make things better.

It sometimes happened, but not often, that a draftsman suggested an idea or even a shape. Most of the time Le Corbusier, somewhat annoyed, rejected them right away. He could not bear to have someone interfere, and if he finally adopted the suggestion it was in a rethought way. He would draw it again and reintegrate it into the unity of the whole. He was the sole author of all the projects I saw being born.

All of that in no way contradicts his unquestionable need to have good assistants to whom he entrusted much of the work and who extended his own work by transforming his drawings into final drawings, working out the technical details, representing him at innumerable meetings, and supervising the building sites. He needed Charlotte Perriand to create the furniture prototypes and supervise their manufacture. Before 1939, he did everything with his cousin and associate Pierre Jeanneret, a man of great qualities who represented him again, after the war, at Chandigarh. After 1945, he would have done nothing without his team of faithful, dynamic young men. He knew that. At the opening of the *Unité* at Marseilles he ended his speech with an emotional reference to them: "It is to them that I give thanks."

The Drawing Hand

The hand drew, but it did not draw on a flat surface. To engrave is to draw in three dimensions. It means to dig into things or to make them jut out, to see the volume, and the volume can be found both inside and outside.

He drew a shell.

> Tenderness
> Shells the sea has never stopped
> To throw us the joyful, harmonious remains
> Over its shores.
> The hand molds, the hand caresses
> The hand runs its fingers over them. The hand and
> The shell love each other.[29]

The inside is not empty. It is actually the seed, like the sap inside the tree and inside the bud. It is where we find life inside the shell, its place of birth and growth.

Then, cautiously, the drawing hand put human life inside the shape.

Envelope

The hand drew the envelope.

Most tactfully, it drew it around the woman and the man. It enveloped their shapes and measurements. It did not only envelop them motionless but it also surrounded their gestures, their movements, and their actions. It enveloped their thoughts. It was a membrane surrounding them and the children they raised. The envelope is not an arbitrary shape. Rather, it is formed by the life that it surrounds, just as the shell is. The enveloping hand drew the house. The external shape resulted from the life inside.

House and Sun

The house is not separate from the space that surrounds it. It is thrown into the landscape and enveloped by it, and the forces in that landscape also affect the shape of the house. A boundary between the life inside and the life outside, it is shaped by them both. The house is an envelope that is both closed and open. It protects from the outside, but it also opens the interior to it. It connects the two. It establishes a continuity between a given interior and its exterior.

The house is in the light that it receives, in the sun.

"A revolving machine, since time immemorial always on time, it gives birth at every moment of the twenty-four hours to gradations, nuances, to the imperceptible, almost giving them a measure. But it brutally breaks it twice a day, in the morning and in the evening. Continuity belongs to it but it also imposes upon us an alternation—night and day—the two times that regulate our destinies: the sun rises, the sun sets, the sun rises again."[30]

Unity

Under the light, in the air, with plants and living beings, the house is not an isolated thing. It is necessary to have other houses for other men, women, and children, many others. And the hand that drew, the hand led by the mind, plunged into the design of successive envelopes that integrated each other and traced society's image, its social units, on the ground as well as in space, each one the envelope of the cells it contained, the organization of men on earth, an image thought and made concrete of society itself. Unity.

Le Corbusier's hand drew the family home integrated into the *Unité d'Habitation* and the *Unité d'Habitation* integrated into the Radiant City. The industrial units were integrated into the Linear City and crossroads cities were integrated into the region and united by the four roads and by industrial linear cities. Agricultural units were placed inside bypasses, and so on, all the way to the regions and the countries united by the great exchanges. Successive forms, linking and being linked at the same time, open and closed, starting from shells, seeds, bits of life, all the way to the great human forms drawn all over the planet, following the rhythm of night and day.

Radiant City

Le Corbusier was not only an artist. He was an architect almost in spite of himself. But as he was, after all, an architect, he wanted to be a total architect. He could not accept that the functional aspects of architecture be neglected. More than with any other contemporary architect, his architecture rested on a sociological vision. He looked.

He saw that society was structured like an organism, with forms that encompassed and were encompassed, integrated into each other: individuals, families, and increasingly larger social groups. Intuitively, he gathered all the powerful ties that integrate those social forms inside an organic unit. He also collapsed the interaction existing between social structure and architectural structure. He thought and drew town plans and architectures that stemmed from and responded to social structures in order to reinforce their structuring: an organization that created a living organism.

The main idea behind the *Unité d'Habitation* is to isolate the family inside the dwelling in order to protect its privacy (to not see nor hear one's neighbors and to know that they do not see nor hear us), then to reconcile such isolation with the necessary relations with the community. The idea is to reject any conflict between individual and society and to offer an architecture that reconciles individual, family, and community life. It is to go beyond a quantitative juxtaposition of dwellings set against each other, a juxtaposition that remains purely mathematical, in order to integrate the dwellings inside units and freely allow for the development of cultural and functional ties, just as the houses of a small village constitute a community.[31]

Le Corbusier's vision extended beyond the *Unités* to include the city. His city was made of *Unités d'Habitation* that allowed for high density and freed up the ground, of which only ten percent was to be built on. The remainder was a park where nature entered the city. To walk in this city was to walk in a garden.

He avoided the risk of segregating the *Unités d'Habitation* by connecting them all to a center, to an urban heart.

The links toward that center of gravity were provided by places devoted to collective activities, especially to places where thoughts are shared, places for religious rites, culture centers devoted to art and creative endeavors.

He called his city the "Radiant City." His entire vision regarding housing and the city was based on integration. It was a biological vision.

The Radiant City has never been fully carried out. It is surprising and upsetting to realize that out of all of the new towns built in France after the war, whose planning was drawn up as if nothing had changed for a century, our successive leaders have not had the courage to carry out a Radiant City, not even as an experiment, not even at the scale of a city neighborhood. The risk would not have been that great, and the *Unités* built at Marseilles, Rezé-les-Nantes, Berlin, Briey, and Firminy remain isolated prototypes, disembodied limbs severed from the organism that should have given them life.

A country that does not take advantage of the worth of its creators makes an impoverishing mistake both materially and culturally.

Are the *Unités d'Habitation* successful? All objective inquiries and inhabitants' accounts point to their success.

The Other Architect

I think that Auguste Perret did not like his colleagues very much, and yet he approved of the *Unité* at Marseilles. It was Georges Candilis who told me this story.

Auguste Perret came to visit the building site when it was already at a very advanced stage. Candilis welcomed him. They walked through the building. Perret visited the model apartment. He did not say anything beyond some unclear, inarticulate murmurs. They went back down. At the exit of the building site, Auguste Perret, ever his majestic self, turned towards Candilis and told him, "It's good. It's good. After all, there are only two architects. The other one is Le Corbusier."

History

Le Corbusier has been accused of wiping the slate clean in relation to the past. It only shows that his work, both written and projected, is not known in depth, or that there is a lack of objectivity. He loved and wanted to protect the works of the past that had preserved their beauty and spirit, but he rejected the extreme conservationism that wants to preserve a work just because of its old age.

He gave up the Voisin Plan because it was too theoretical, and he himself was critical of it. He made public his true plan for Paris in 1937. It was the plan shown at the Pavillon des Temps Nouveaux at Porte Maillot as part of the International Exposition in Paris. The 1937 plan preserves all the monuments of value, all of historical Paris, the little historical Paris at the heart of the great Paris of outdated town planning and architecture.

Of all the architects I have met, Le Corbusier was the one with the broadest knowledge of the history of architecture. His knowledge was less bookish, less analytical, less external than historians have. It was an understanding he had arrived at not just through the eyes but also with his hands, as it had been engraved on his memory by all the sketches he made in museums and above all during his travels, from his youth to his last trip to Chandigarh.

He told me one day how he had felt with his hand—always that hand complementing the eye—the progressive curve of the fallen Doric capital at the base of the Parthenon. He then drew its outline from memory.

On another occasion, he asked me if I knew any books on Brunelleschi. He wanted to study his life and work, which he loved.

He knew the architecture of the past very well, even from those periods he did not like very much. Early in 1937, while he prepared the Pavillon des Temps Nouveaux, he asked me to draw a great view of Paris as seen from a plane (not too much to ask!) to show the four business towers where he was to centralize all office space and to show as well that all of historical Paris was preserved. He mistakenly thought that a young Beaux-Arts student like me would be highly accomplished in all types of perspective drawing. It was necessary to draw a small Panthéon from a corner on high on the right-hand side. I mumbled. Le Corbusier arrived. "What? A Beaux-Arts student like you, is that the way you know classical architecture?" And he started drawing in great detail the whole of the Panthéon, showing me how Soufflot had planned the columns, the pediment, the cornice, and the drum. He had the Panthéon in his eyes and in his hand.

How can one not feel in his built and projected work the influence of the architecture history has left behind, above all, that of ancient Egypt and Rome, both of them so particularly dear to him?

Universal

Could it be that Le Corbusier's architecture has not yet allowed for enough hindsight? It never fell into the trap of passing fashions. It did not want to please the fleeting taste of the moment. It placed itself in time beyond fashions and styles. It rediscovered great human values, those that are permanent and universal, beyond space and time. Once the passionate arguments for and against, the rivalries, jealousies, and ideologies have calmed down, I am convinced that Le Corbusier's architecture will find a good place in the history of architecture.

Indeed, there exist, deep inside the human soul, profound, permanent, universal values.

In our travels, if we do not pay too much attention to the exceptional and we observe what is permanent and fundamental, we can't help but grasp the following truth: there exist among men all over the planet many more similarities than differences.

If we are moved by the beauty and the poetry of the frescoes at Lascaux, the falcon of Horus from Edfu, the temples at Karnak or at Deir-el-Bahari, the sculpted mountain top at Monte Albán, the stone garden of the Rioanji temple in Kyoto, the abbey at Thoronet, or the Villa Savoye, it is because there exist deep inside the human species, throughout time and space, fundamental, permanent, universal values.

The making of art is an attempt to rediscover them, reveal them, and perpetuate them. Le Corbusier's architecture expresses such values.

As in a Mozart concerto, the Villa Savoye and the General Assembly building at Chandigarh were for Le Corbusier prodigious acts of surpassing the personal toward the universal.

Functionalism

It has often been said that Le Corbusier was a rationalist or a functionalist architect. *A priori* one might take that as a compliment, since obviously an architecture worthy of such a beautiful name should be a response to function and to practical problems and should be studied with intelligence.

It is correct to think that Le Corbusier gave considerable importance to practical problems in opposition to a deficient architecture that neglected them to concern itself solely with decoration. He was not the only one. Early in the twentieth century architecture was in great need of that.

Le Corbusier wanted an architecture resulting from the activities performed inside a building. As the envelope of movements, actions, and thoughts, he tried to shape his architecture according to those movements, actions, and thoughts. Indeed, he wanted a spatial organization that was rational, intelligent, and conducive to the development of life. He did not like wasting space at all. He had a sense of "economy" of space in the same way that "economy" is referred to in human exchanges and relations.

But he hated the terms "functionalism" and "rationalism" because he feared that they would be turned into limits or rules for architecture. He said that it was foolish to believe that "what is functional is of necessity beautiful" as certain architects wanted to have it.

In 1931, he turned down A. Sartoris's request to write a preface to one of the latter's books on functionalism. He replied him so: "For me, the term architecture has something more magical about it than rational or functional…."[32]

To limit his work to this utilitarian aspect is like seeing only one tree when we are inside a forest. It means not seeing the hand working with space like the musician works with duration and time, the hand trying to take architecture beyond what is rational to the threshold of aesthetic emotion.

Machine

In order to understand Le Corbusier, we must look deeply into his intentions, his secret desires, and understand them, even examine them beyond words.

His famous saying, "a house is a machine for living in," has harmed him greatly. Many have not understood it; some have not wanted to understand it. Yet, "let's all put into our heads once and for all that a chair is a machine to sit on. A house is a machine for living in.... A tree is a machine to carry fruit. A plant is a machine to carry flowers and seeds.... A heart is a suction pump."[33] This quote is not Le Corbusier's but Frank Lloyd Wright's.

The general public is afraid of the word "machine." Yet it dreams of owning more and more increasingly perfected machines. The car, which must always be more sophisticated than previous models and faster than them, even too fast, is more of a status symbol than the home. We always want more modern appliances. We admire technical performance more and more, but our houses must be old or give the impression of being old.

Le Corbusier was right in having faith in the machine or, more precisely, in its potential. He wanted to see the house as technically developed as a car or a plane, with the same kind of performance. Despite his interest in performance, he did not at all exclude that which remained his main goal: spatial beauty and spatial poetry. There was no contradiction.

Utopia

Le Corbusier is also accused of being utopian.

If that is meant in the original and strict sense of the word, that is to say, "that which cannot be found anywhere," it is correct. No project by Le Corbusier, not even Chandigarh, represents the sum total of his ideas and proposals. In the original sense, however, the term does not mean unfeasible.

If the word is taken in its pejorative sense, meaning "unviable," I do not think that the term utopian applies to Le Corbusier. His intuition and his imagination were full of lucidity. The success of his built works, the considerable influence of his oeuvre in the twentieth century, all these results come to show that his ideas are viable and that his oeuvre is a success.

In the case of a true utopian, the inventor takes the place of the artist. Le Corbusier walked the fine line that separates the ideal from the utopian. He knew what point of perfection he was allowed to reach without going too far. I believe that Le Corbusier was first of all a realist, but by the power of his creative force he directed that realism toward an ideal. His works were first of all thought out in relation to what contemporary people are, as individuals, families, and societies. All of his architecture and town planning were based on a vision of social structures. He did not, however, just take them as they were. He measured the limits to which he could lead them on his way toward a possible ideal.[34]

It was one of his great strengths. His imagination was never gratuitous. He thought about men, women, and children before thinking about architecture, which for him was only a means to an end.

When he returned from his first trip to the future site of Chandigarh, I went to the airport to welcome him. His first words were, "Out there, Wogenscky, we will do a very different town planning." I was disappointed. I had envisioned the Radiant City at the foot of the Himalayas. I asked him why. "Because out there, in the evening, people carry their beds on their backs and go to sleep outside."

Progress

Le Corbusier believed in the possibility of progress. He took part in that movement of ideas at the beginning of the twentieth century that trusted science and technology.

Le Corbusier was harshly criticized, and still is, for this way of seeing his time period. His detractors accuse him of having been excessively naive, of having taken part in the sort of conviction that caught the imagination of so many people during the first half of the twentieth century: the possibilities offered by the development of science and technology would give a great boost to humanity in the construction of that happiness human beings never tire of pursuing.

I do not believe such criticisms are justified if we take the context of the period into account. Le Corbusier expressed certain wishes. He showed that in the years preceding World War II, mankind, particularly the West, found itself expectant. It was necessary to choose. There existed the possibility of considering that period as a period of renewal, one that would reconstruct society and create a better face for humankind, with greater justice and hope for the future.

"There is a new spirit. A great era has just started."[35]

He could see the evidence for such possibilities for progress everywhere except in architecture. "There is one profession, only one, architecture, where progress is not prescribed, where laziness reigns, where they talk about yesterday."[36]

Faced with all these possibilities, he would have liked our time period to resemble the Middle Ages. Since that was what he wanted, he claimed that, "It was once similar in every respect, seven centuries ago, while a new world was being born, when the cathedrals were white."[37]

Science, technology, and the machine are nothing, however. It all depends on what use mankind makes of them. That implies a choice, an intention, a will, and a passionate engagement.

"Greatness exists in the intention, not at all in the dimension. When the cathedrals were white, the whole universe was stirred up by an immense faith in action, in the future, and in the harmonious creation of a civilization."[38]

All architecture, like the architecture of cathedrals, reflects the intention with which it was born. It is all a question of human beings.

"Those among them brave enough will penetrate the thickness of architecture, that all-encompassing profession, scorned today by the Schools and their degrees, that profession that imposes implacable servitudes, from real estate honesty (on a philosophical level) to the most refined imagination. It is controlled by the laws of physics, at the service of sociology, brutalized by economic factors, often enslaved by politics, and so on—a formidable battle out of which the face of modern times will emerge and during which aesthetic and artistic aspirations will find their expression, the most modest as well as the loftiest one, in the exactness of everyday endeavors forever fraught with exhausting conflicts.

That art period is emerging, and it is on this newly turned page that will be drawn not only pictorial abstractions, painted on canvas and framed, but also a formal synthesis, born and made on the job, by ordinary people, people attached to, associated to, totally devoted to the building: a new generation capable of sacrificing its security and its pleasure in order to become soldiers for the given task, all over the world, through the construction of this same world."[39]

Space

When he drew spatial forms, Le Corbusier placed them in an isotropic space.

I was very interested in Einstein's relativity theory and read books to try to understand something about it. I talked about it with Le Corbusier twice or three times, but he swerved around the question. Minkowski's space-time continuum did not mean anything to him. For him, space was motionless, homogeneous, isotropic, and inert. I had the impression that I was boring him. He seemed to think that all of that had no interest for architects.

Yet he was very sensitive to the forces operating in a given site, above all the sun making certain directions more important than others. He never grew tired of drawing the 24-hour solar-cycle curve and the alternation of day and night. In his sketches he took note of the views, the contours, the differences in value that different directions can have when we study a plot of land. He was sensitive to earthly and cosmic forces. I think, however, that even if he thought such forces existed and moved across space, for him they were not space itself.

His idea of space was the same as Brunelleschi's and, as such, as with many other aspects, he was classical, one could almost say ancient.

Yet his architecture is often dynamic, loaded with forces and rhythms.

"Around the building, inside the building there are precisely defined places, mathematical places that integrate the whole and that are like platforms from which the voice of a speech will find its echo all around it. Such are the places for statues. And it will not be a metope, a tympanum, or a porch. It is far more precise and subtle. It is a place like the focal point of a parabola or an ellipse, like the exact place where the different planes that compose the architectural landscape intersect. These are voice-bearing places, mouthpieces, loudspeakers."[40]

However, his architecture remains an architecture thought in an isotropic space. It is not space itself that is dynamic and relative. It remains a kind of inert container, unlimited and abstract. Le Corbusier, who was not at all a mathematician, maintained a view of space that was theoretical and mathematical: homogeneous, inert, neutral, and inanimate. It was the architecture that animated the space.

Is it possible that it could be otherwise? Perhaps. Among architects at the end of this century I believe that some, surely just a few, try to operate a mutation. Before they think the architecture up, they try to think of an anisotropic space, one that is relative, non-homogeneous, and made up of energy fields. The architecture has to mold itself in this space, adopt its dynamism or try to transform it. It is not only the architecture that creates energy in the space. The very space receiving the architecture is an energy field conditioning it. Will this kind of mutation of the spatial conception perhaps one day result in an architecture in four dimensions, in a time-architecture continuum?

Form

Le Corbusier's hand drew shapes in three dimensions. They were volumes, volumetric because they were containers, for architecture is an envelope. For all the human complexities that it envelops, however, architecture does not take on complex or sophisticated forms. It brings this complexity back to simple, primary forms, the forms of elementary geometry: the cube, the cylinder, the prism, at times the nondevelopable curve, portions of the sphere, at times the form limited by a warped surface. Simple volumes can contain all complexities, while complicated forms cannot contain simplicity. The simple form is preferred because the disorder of a chaotic world is clarified and appeased by such architecture.

His hand never drew arbitrary forms. From the dialogue between the hand and the mind always resulted a thought-out form, a form that had very good reasons to be as it was, with roots that penetrated people's lives, be they individual, in couples, in families, or in society. They are forms organized not only for human action but even more so for human thoughts; forms that are not only functional, but whose organization is also pushed to the level of artistic beauty. Le Corbusier's highest aspiration: beautiful forms.

Beautiful

One day his hand drew a square, but it was a round square. It was something between a square and a circle: a square whose corners were rounded, a circle some of whose opposing arcs had been flattened out. He told me that he liked that flat shape and that he found it beautiful depending on the exactness that one gave it. It was not any old shape between a square and a circle. It was precisely proportioned according to the gesture of the hand, a sort of right balance found in the swing that goes back and forth between the square and the circle.

That complex space brought back to simple forms is enriched by the imbrication of these forms. To put them together is to establish an exchange between them and a link, a passage from one to the other. The flow goes from cube to cylinder and back, going beyond the juxtaposition that is nothing other than independence and inertia between neighboring forms, but putting them together so that one plus one can make one, and so that several can still make one. It is an impulse between them that allows us to see our own life impulse.

A shape is beautiful because it is an image of our thinking, an impulse that tries to express our aspirations. The act of thinking, however, runs the risk of fading into the incorporeal fluidity of thoughts. Architecture, like all arts, turns the form that has been thought into something corporeal. The thought is made concrete. The more the thought is intense and profound, the more the architectural form is beautiful.

Void

The beautiful shapes drawn by Le Corbusier were not only the full, concrete, closed shapes, but also the voids. The shape of the voids was thought in the same way as the shape of the filled-in parts. They complemented each other. The void was not a residual part. It was also architecture. Sometimes it was even more loaded with meaning than the full form merely serving as its envelope. In the "villa-apartments" of the *Unités d'Habitation,* it is the void that has a positive form. That is also the case in the hall of the Assembly in Chandigarh, in the corridors of the monastery of La Tourette, and inside its church. The Villa Savoye continues to be one of the most beautiful works by Le Corbusier for many reasons: one of them is the extraordinary balance between full and empty volumes—the rigorous complementarity between them—where the void is a positive form inside the envelope defining it.

The importance given to the void fills the architecture with meaning since it is when we succeed at creating a void in our inner life that we can experience it in its fullness, in all its richness and fecundity.

"We work the clay in the shape of a vase, for it is precisely where there is nothing that the effectiveness of the vase resides. We make openings for doors and windows to make a house, for it is precisely where there is nothing that the effectiveness of the house resides. Thus, we think that we benefit from things that are tangible, but it is precisely where we do not perceive anything that the true effectiveness resides."[41]

Skin

The beauty of the shapes drawn by Le Corbusier's hand is not only perceived by the eye, but also by the touch. It also involves the viewer's hand. Le Corbusier studied with great care the materials with which he had his forms made and the textures that those forms offered to our sense of touch and sight.

During the thirty years I knew him, he wanted to build with steel frameworks as well as with carefully studied components, industrially manufactured and assembled at the building site. When I was his assistant, comparative studies were often made between steel frameworks and reinforced concrete. Every time, according to the results provided by the engineers, reinforced concrete was found to be much cheaper and we made do with that. Only the Centre Le Corbusier in Zurich, which was a project to be manufactured industrially, was built in metal.

While studying reinforced concrete, Le Corbusier learned to love it. Since his youth he had admired the first concrete constructions. Later he understood that its texture could be as beautiful as the texture of stone.

He loved concrete that could take any shape, as it was molded in forms. He studied the molding forms so that the surface, the skin, did not come out in any old way but animated by the imprint of the mold, which it had kept in a solidified form. In the *Unité d'Habitation* at Marseilles he used, for the first time, "unmolded" rough concrete poured in wooden forms so that the concrete could retain their imprint.

He played with the contrast of materials between rough and smooth, warm and cold. He loved wood, which he called "man's friend." He pushed the study of forms to their very skin. "I believe in the skin of things as in the skin of women."[42]

When we look at his architecture, we follow it with our eyes just as we would with our hand. He himself felt it with his hand and in his hand while he was drawing it. Now, as we cover it with our eyes, we would like to have a very large hand that could touch it, spread our fingers over it and take it, perceive the play of forms in our palm and between our fingers, under the caress of our skin over the skin of its forms.

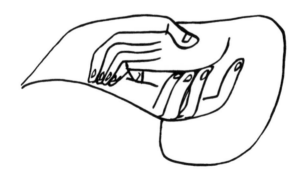

A Gift

Architectural forms are like human beings; they can be beautiful or ugly, strong or weak, violent or gentle, aggressive or soothing. Le Corbusier's architecture is always strong, just as his hand was strong. Sometimes it is violent, but it is rarely aggressive, and almost always it is gentle and tender. Architecture is like people; only those who are strong can be calm and gentle.

"What is wonderful about a house is not that it shelters you and keeps you warm, nor that you own its walls, but that it slowly leaves in you a good supply of gentleness."[43]

Who can say how large the reserve of tenderness that we can draw from the Villa Savoye is?

The beauty of architecture is a generous gift. We can take it, make it ours, and carry it with us. It will not be diminished by this. It is inexhaustible. Someone else can come after us and receive it and take it along as we did.

This is all because the shapes drawn by Le Corbusier's hand and conceived by him call us. If we don't shut up our thinking, they come toward us. When we find his architecture beautiful, it is not just that we like it. It is the architecture that seems to like us.

Nungesser and Coli

A street in Paris was named after the two pilots. Le Corbusier and Pierre Jeanneret drew the plans for an apartment building at 24 rue Nungesser et Coli. Le Corbusier turned the seventh floor and the roof garden into his own apartment and painting studio, and I have the great fortune to rent them from the Le Corbusier Foundation to use as my architecture studio.

In this apartment, there are many details that are not functional at all. To go through one of the doors, it is necessary to lower one's head to avoid hitting it against the top. The restrooms are too small. The elevator does not reach the seventh floor. To gain access to the apartment it is necessary to go over a small gangway that is too narrow. The stairs, moreover, turn too tightly and become impassable the moment one carries the smallest load. To move things in and out it is necessary to use a rather dangerous hoist installed over the interior court.

Le Corbusier told me how awful he felt when the first death occurred in one of the apartments. The coffin could not be taken up the stairs. It was necessary to hoist it up and down the court. The family was outraged and Le Corbusier dismayed. Neither he nor Pierre Jeanneret had anticipated that!

All these inconveniences, however, are rather minor when compared with the riches provided by the architecture. In his large painting studio Le Corbusier left the party wall of the neighboring building exposed. It is made of limestone blocks. On the right, we see the brick fireplace incorporated into the wall. It is a living vertical surface. The studio, the living room, and the bedroom are covered with white vaults. The low ceilings are faced with wood. The walls are white. The proportions are similar to those of humans. The forms are hand-made. One might even think Le Corbusier made them with his own hands. We work under the sweet pressure of his architecture.

In the bedroom, the shape of the shower and the formal play resemble the kinds of vernacular architecture built without architects. Yet the proportions have been wisely studied, and also made simple. I slept there several nights. One feels like a child who loves to be cuddled to sleep.

Such interior architecture is made of silence. Silence is not the total absence of sound, but the absolute calmness we obtain for the ear. Here silence is given to our eyes.

My drawing board is in the living room, next to the dining table in marble designed by Le Corbusier. I sit at my drawing board. I don't move for several minutes. I let the white vault descend slowly around me. It helps me enter inside myself. It supports me. It seems to me that it stops me from falling. It is present and at the same time it slowly disappears. It leaves me free. It has placed me on that measured level where the necessary mystery for the imagination exists. Then I start drawing.

His Mother

Le Corbusier once told me one of the most cherished memories of his family life: his mother playing Händel at the piano with his brother playing the violin.

His mother lived to be a hundred years old. One day, she came to visit the building site of the *Unité d'Habitation* at Marseilles. She was almost ninety years old at the time. She arrived with Le Corbusier's elder brother, Albert Jeanneret. The three of them went all over the site accompanied by our small team. The elevator had not yet been installed. She went up stairs that did not yet have railings and up some ladders. Her two sons were over sixty. She talked to them as if they were still her little boys.

At night they slept in the model apartment. She slept in the master bedroom and the two sons slept in the two small bedrooms for children. Before going to bed, we gathered in the living room. Night closed in over the trees. The conversation floated hesitantly. We were all shy. Le Corbusier was silent. I loved looking at his face as it turned towards his mother.

I believe that through his architecture Le Corbusier, perhaps unknowingly, looked to satisfy more or less completely a deep maternal need.

Light

A memory: Le Corbusier was drawing. A shape was born from his hand. He showed the assistants around him that the shape was only visible because of its lit side, its own shadow and the shadow it carried. His architecture is always a play of shadows and light created by architectural forms.[44]

He traveled around the Mediterranean. He loved it because of its light. In Turkey, in Greece, in the Mzab, the shape of the house is the luminous envelope of the life inside. To see it is to perceive the sun in the cosmos. The house is a link between life and the universe.

As he organized the forms in a rigorous order, as he set them up according to the right angle, the horizontal and the vertical, as he measured the proportions and created rhythms in space, as he upset the order by introducing a diagonal or a curve, an unexpected shape, a color, he made the nuances of light play with the nuances of shadows. The light is very bright, or softened, dim, or altogether gone.

Each morning his architecture comes to life again in the elongated shadows, in a warm light. It bursts at noon in the contrasts of the shadows. It dies a bit every evening, as the night covers it all, to be born again the following day in the light.

Modulor

The young Le Corbusier, who drew from books in libraries and sketched in museums, who traveled with his backpack letting his hand draw all that he saw, became aware through his drawing of the extreme importance of proportions. They are the primordial basis of beauty. He developed a passion for regulating lines. He drew many of them to find the correspondences between points, between lines. The points and lines that establish the outline of the forms could not be placed at random. The regulating lines allowed for a rigorous composition. Neither could dimensions be allowed to relate to one another at random. They had to be exactly related and to have the only correct relation they could have.

Referring to a man who was no other than himself, Le Corbusier explained:

"One day, there were postcards spread over the table under an oil lamp in his small room in Paris. The image of Michelangelo's Capitol in Rome caught his eye. He turned another postcard blank face up and he intuitively moved it to one of the angles (right angle) on the facade of the Capitol. Suddenly, an acceptable truth became apparent: the right angle regulated the composition. That was a revelation, a certainty. The same test worked on a painting by Cézanne, but our man did not trust his verdict and told himself: the composition of works of art is arranged according to rules. These rules can be subtle, conscious, or ostensible methods. They can also be clichéd and banal. They can also result from the creative instinct of the artist, as manifestations of an intuitive harmony, an example of which we can almost surely find in Cézanne. Michelangelo had a different nature and was prone to erudite, preconceived, deliberate lines."[45]

He studied the books of Matila Ghyka and developed a passion for the golden section.

Later he came up with the idea of installing a grid on the building site, next to the construction.

"I dream of installing on the building sites that will later cover the whole country a proportional grid drawn on the wall or placed against the wall, made of welded iron strips. It will be the rule of the site, the yardstick that will open an unlimited series of combinations and proportions. The mason, the carpenter, the joiner will go to it time and again to choose the measurements of their work and all these diverse and different tasks will testify to the rule of harmony. Such is my dream."

"Take a man with his outstretched arm pointing up (2.20 meters tall). Place him inside two overlapping squares measuring 1.10 meters. Superimpose a third square over the two squares and that will give you the solution. The place of the right angle should help you position the third square correctly. With this proportional grid for building sites applied to the measurements of the human being living inside, I am convinced that you will come up with a sequence of measurements that will find an agreement between human height (with a raised arm) and mathematics...."[46]

Strangely, here reappears the influence of the hand, of manual work, of vernacular housing. He, who had envisioned and wished for a vast industrialization of construction methods; he, who made us prepare numerous, very detailed, very precise drawings where virtually everything had been contemplated in advance; was he now willing to ask for the mason's and the joiner's advice? Yes, all right, he liked talking to them and learning from them, but he would have been furious if a worker or an engineer made a decision regarding a formal matter. Everything had to be designed by him, Le Corbusier, or controlled by him. Was this paradoxical? Maybe.

Contradictory? Maybe not. The prototypes that are the basis of industrialized construction, before they can be serially produced, should be finalized according to all the possibilities provided by science and technology, but also according to the riches provided by manual work, by the touch of forms, the gestures of one's fingers, palms, and arms. The hand is still present and active.

Le Corbusier then got together a small team to assist him with the study of his grid. I was fortunate to be a member of this team along with Aujame, Hanning, de Looze, and Soltan. He consulted Mademoiselle Maillart, the curator of the Cluny Museum in Paris and a great specialist in regulating lines.

Le Corbusier, Mademoiselle Maillart, and Hanning became more and more immersed in the idea of "the place of the right angle." Mademoiselle Maillart and Hanning drew with a certain lack of precision that led to errors of interpretation. Some of us told Le Corbusier, but he was not confident enough. He consulted some mathematicians: Andreas Speiser, professor at Zurich University, and Dean Montel, professor at the School of Sciences in Paris. The latter told him, "From the moment you were able to place the right angle inside the double square, you introduced the $\sqrt{5}$ function thus provoking a profusion of golden sections."

Although the right angle was incorrectly placed inside the double square, the study led to the golden section. To Le Corbusier's great surprise it ended far away from the building site grid and in the two Fibonacci sequences constituting the double scale of the Modulor.

The two series were established taking the measurement 1.78 meters, the standard height of a man (2.20 meters, if his arm is raised), as their point of departure. One day one of Le Corbusier's collaborators arrived triumphantly: he had figured out that, starting with a man 1.83 meters tall, one could find many correspondences between the Modulor and the English measuring system (feet and inches). Le Corbusier was delighted. He dreamed of reconciling the English system with the metric system so that the Modulor could become a universal tool.

Without wanting to, I started a passionate debate. I pointed out that even if the Modulor was a wonderful instrument for establishing proportions and dimensions, it was not a measuring tool since Le Corbusier himself continued to use the metric system to define the dimensions determined by the Modulor. Le Corbusier was not happy and I was snubbed. He kept on calling the Modulor a measuring tool.

Who cares! The Modulor is a very rich instrument that helps perfect proportions, just as a piano tuner finds the exact relation between sounds. Einstein put it very nicely when Le Corbusier met him at Princeton: "It's a tool that makes the good easy and the bad difficult."

Based at the same time on mathematical properties and on the human body, the Modulor keeps architecture on the human scale, the container of man's movements and actions, an affirmation in space of the horizontal planes of his feet, hands, and vision.

Music

The successive play of forms in space, their proportions, their dimensions, create rhythms not unlike those created by music in time. Architecture is spatial music.

"The plan establishes the hold that the human being will have on space. We cover the plan on foot, eyes looking ahead. Our perception of space is successive and it involves time. We perceive a sequence of visual events, just as a symphony is a sequence of sound events. Time, duration, succession, and continuity are the constituent factors of architecture. That cancels out and condemns star-shaped plans, and denounces as a result centuries of decadence and degeneration. Plan and section turn architecture into the sister art of music."[47]

The facades of the *Unités d'Habitation* are beautiful examples of those visual rhythms. They have a double rhythm, vertical and horizontal at the same time. The width of the apartments, measuring 3.66 meters each, creates a series of equal spans that establishes a basic horizontal rhythm. That cadence is crossed perpendicularly by a more complex vertical rhythm created by the play of the loggias of single or double height, which itself is in turn intersected by the cadence of the horizontal bands of the balustrades. The facade is vertical music.

The building of the Secretariat in Chandigarh is another example of this kind of rhythmic play.

A memory: following the sketches Le Corbusier had made, I made the drawings of the Claude et Duval hosiery factory that he was building in Saint-Dié. The columns of the structural framework were inserted in the glass paneling. The distance between them established a cadence on a vertical plane. The glass paneling created another vertical plane that, on its external side, had sunbreakers made of vertical slabs. They were three vertical planes highlighted by vertical lines. In my naiveté, I tried to come up with a common measure between the intercolumniation of the pillars, the distance between the jambs of the glass paneling, and the distance separating the vertical sunbreakers. I could not find it. Le Corbusier came to my drawing board and showed me that it was not necessary to look for a common measure. It was a matter of giving each one of those distances its proper size. So much the better if the result was not perfect! The verticals were not in front of each other. There would be a discrepancy. There would be a visual counterpoint.

"Music, like architecture, is time and space."[48]

Color is also a musical factor, a melody introduced into the rhythm or an accompaniment supporting the melody. One day, when we were studying the *Unité d'Habitation* for Marseilles, I suggested that Le Corbusier paint the interior of the loggias. I was happy because he thought it was a good idea. He worked out the polychromy with meticulous care. He then got his team together and explained what the difficulty was: it was necessary to prevent the colors from linking up visually thus creating lines and patterns over the facades. If they were placed at random, that was the result, as when the stars form constellations. It was necessary to give the impression that the colors had been randomly placed, and that was the most difficult part. He also explained that the colors had to be only inside the loggias so that the external vertical plane remained unaltered. In the end, however, I was disappointed by the colors he used.

As in music, silences are part of the architectural rhythm. They become very important. Not only the voids and the shape of the voids, but also blank surfaces, solid walls, the breaks in rhythm, the large open spaces.

"Music is not the opposite of silence but its complement. When Indians play music, they hide because they know that music, even more dangerously than language, leaves them exposed."[49]

Contemporary musicians talk about the "volume of sound." Architects could talk about "visible durations."

In music, rhythm is like something motionless that has been made to move. In architecture, it is like immobilized movement.

Poetry

In that strange dialogue between Le Corbusier's hand, his thinking, and his whole being, beauty did not suffice for the drawing hand and the reflective mind.

Ordered, structured, with correct proportions and rhythms, architecture could be beautiful but also cold, static, inert. Le Corbusier's hand, guided by his mind, went beyond that. It disrupted that beauty and projected it into the realm of poetry. Although his architecture was completely thought out in advance, structured, seen by him in his mind before it was built, Le Corbusier loved accidents in his architecture. Sometimes he loved mistakes in the construction. I would often have to beg him not to tell the contractors. He loved accidents—that which could not be foreseen—which introduced an element of randomness in the formal order and disrupted its organization.

At Marseilles, on the roof garden, the coating covering the waterproofing on the vault of the gym started to crack. As I had been told to forbid the repair of any fault in the construction before Le Corbusier had seen it, I asked the contractor to wait for Le Corbusier to come. I was not proud of the cracking. Le Corbusier came. He was delighted. He showed me the beauty of the graphic signs drawn on the vault by the lines of the cracks. He ordered me to get a brush and bright red paint, and paint a red line following the cracks exactly. It was not a joke. The red lines were drawn and they stayed on the gym for some time. Unfortunately, it was eventually necessary to reapply the coating!

Once it had put order into something, Le Corbusier's drawing hand disrupted that order to go beyond its beauty and reach the level of poetry. The poetry of a diagonal line rightly placed in a play of orthogonal lines, the contrast between a curve and a cube, the poetry of a curve that was rigorous and soft at the same time, soft as a result of its rigor. The exception inserted in a proportional system. "To make presences emerge in the built work (architecture) that provoke emotions, essential factors in the phenomenon of poetry."[50]

To animate architecture, to make it feasible, to give it life, such was Le Corbusier's true goal.

In his *Poem of the Right Angle,* he wrote: "to make architecture is to make a living being."[51]

Becoming

Le Corbusier's life was a continuum. From the Villa La Roche of 1923 to the chapel at Ronchamp and his church project for Firminy, from the Villa Savoye to the Capitol at Chandigarh, there is continuity. Seemingly Ronchamp is smoother, less rigid than the Villa Savoye, but if we open up to the architecture we will find an extraordinary rigor both at Ronchamp and in the Firminy church, a tremendous amount of tenderness in the Villa Savoye, and great softness in the double curve of the project for a congress hall at Strasbourg.

All his life is a continuum. When we leaf through his seventy-four sketchbooks we find remarkable continuity and unity. We might say of him: "He is not, he becomes."

Human beings can be divided into two tendencies. The large majority remain locked in the past. They produce nothing but imitation and the degradation of what they imitate. The others, a minority, are fully involved in an effort to understand the present—to prepare for tomorrow and reveal it.

"It is better to grow green again than to stay green forever."[52]

Le Corbusier positioned himself facing the times that were coming.

"Trackers place themselves facing the times that come. Usually we look at time as it moves away from us. Only trackers can modify that and fix time as it moves toward them."[53]

To the last moment, the life of Le Corbusier was a process of becoming.

Continuum

His work, that strange two-way exchange between his hand and his mind, was also a continuous process. It was a crescendo. First he received. He took in everything that he saw. He immersed himself in the land on which to build, in the program to follow. He imagined future users and put himself in their place. He forgot himself to be transmuted into them. He let things ripen and held back the forms that wanted to emerge too quickly from his imagination.

That creative process itself went through a number of phases in a similarly continuous manner. First, he used to their fullest capacity all the possibilities offered by intelligence and reason. Le Corbusier wanted an intelligent architecture as well as rigorous mathematical reasoning. He called the skyscraper he proposed for the business center in his 1937 plan for Paris "Cartesian." Yet he wanted to go beyond the rational. As the architectural form was ordered and organized, a formal, aesthetic preoccupation that was to eventually replace rational organization became increasingly important. It was a continuous organizational process. It was a progressive evolution of his thinking from a rational state to an aesthetic state.

Aesthetic State, Poetic State

I have spent years trying to understand what went on in his mind and in his hand.

Sometimes it is said that artists are not aware of what they do. I do not think so. When they create, they are in a state of acute awareness. It is a mental state encompassing the entire potential of reason, but surpassing it. It is a state above the rational. It is the state where we stop searching and we start finding. It is the mental state of great thinkers, great poets, great scientists, and all great creative people. It is the mental state of Einstein, who saw even before he could confirm by calculation. It is what we call intuition because we do not know what it is. It seems that Brancusi once said, "What's difficult is not to make something, but to put oneself in a state conducive to making."[54]

The continuum can go even further. If the creative individuals have enough energy for it, the aesthetic state, tightened up by an immense desire, becomes the poetic state of their minds.

"What that is about is that all of a sudden life is breathed into things."[55]

Emptiness is created in order to fill oneself again. One relaxes to let the creative energy and the impulse of life emerge. It is a kind of trance, but it is not about rolling on the ground shouting. It is about being concentrated but also open, calm but also intense.

"I put myself in a trance. Nobody notices it, but it is so."[56]

The aesthetic and poetic state entails one's transmutation into the created form. It means that one only exists in this form. It is the act of love, for, in truth, one only exists in the object of one's love.

Ineffable Space

For Le Corbusier the goal was to get to and to create an "ineffable space."

"I am the inventor of the phrase 'ineffable space,' which is a reality that I discovered as I went on. When a work reaches a maximum of intensity, when it has the best proportions and has been made with the best quality of execution, when it has reached perfection, a phenomenon takes place that we may call 'ineffable space.' When this happens, these places start to radiate. They radiate in a physical way and determine what I call 'ineffable space,' that is to say, a space that does not depend on dimensions but on the quality of its perfection. It belongs in the domain of the ineffable, of that which cannot be said."[57]

"I do not know the miracle of faith, but I often experience that of ineffable space, which is the highest level of artistic emotion."[58]

It was at that moment that Le Corbusier found joy and transmitted it.

Will someone one day be able to describe the beauty of that life, its hardness, its anxiety, its disappointments, its bitterness and sorrows, its triumphant joy, its need to love and be loved, its need of tenderness, its immense work, and that return to the self so full of generosity?

Perhaps it is necessary to experience those disappointments, that anxiety, and the sadness that comes as a result, in order to overcome them with the energy of the self, and, like Mozart and Le Corbusier, beyond the sadness find joy again and transmit it.

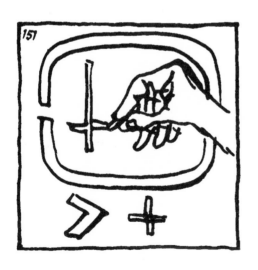

Right Angle

All of Le Corbusier's architecture is based on the right angle. In space, which he considered isotropic, he placed an orthogonal space. All his plans were thought out within this orthogonality. Whenever possible, it followed a North-South axis so it could be installed along the apparent course of the sun or along the strongest direction on the site. The Villa La Roche, the Villa Savoye, the Swiss Pavilion, the 1937 plan for Paris, the plan for Saint-Dié, the *Unités d'Habitation,* the Museum of Western Art in Tokyo, the monastery of La Tourette, the entire Capitol at Chandigarh, his entire oeuvre was a complex play of lines, planes, and volumes brought to a simplicity and a unity made possible by spatial orthogonality. The space that integrated all forms was the right angle and the proliferation of right angles. Curves, diagonals, and soft shapes—all were inscribed within this framework that seemed to contain them with rigor. Even the "Obus" plan for Algiers was based on the right angle as it was centered on the office tower, to which he attached with rigor the exactness of the curves integrated in the landscape.

Volumes were brought to surfaces, brought to lines, and all lines were brought to two lines: vertical and horizontal. Those two lines were brought to a single unity: the right angle.

Even the Ronchamp chapel, which seems to be nothing but a play of curves, is based on the right angle. The right angle is inscribed on the floor with black lines, the longitudinal axis of the nave and the transverse axis that links the northwest and southwest chapels. There, however, the right angle is distorted. Le Corbusier's hand leaned towards the cross axis. It is no longer perpendicular. It is tensed up, bent like a bow. An exact right angle can be static. A distorted right angle is charged with strength. A slack bow is inert. A bent bow is charged with potential energy. A few years later the right angle found its restful state again in the great serene space of the church at La Tourette. Even the shape of the hand: to draw The Open Hand he stretched it to fit the right angle.

For Le Corbusier the right angle was not just architecture. It was the basis of human thought. He liked Mondrian and I believe he was influenced by him, like Rietveld was. He said of Mondrian that he was "an unincarnated architect."[59]

The right angle is human intelligence bringing space toward the vertical line dictated by weight, and toward the horizontal plane along which our eyes move and within which they settle in their search for the infinite. It is the axis of all things, the reference without which we cannot locate anything, especially ourselves. It is the order toward which our thinking process brings all natural forms that are unpredictable, random, and sometimes chaotic. It is the geometrical order in relation to which we look at the world and we think.

The right angle is not just an abstraction. It is the human being itself in nature.

> Our visual universe rests on a plateau lined by a horizon.
> With our face turned toward the sky, let us consider
> The inconceivable space that up until then eluded us.
> To rest, to lie down, to sleep, to die.
> With our back resting on the ground…
> But I stood up!
> Since you are upright,
> You are prone to act.
> Upright on the flat surface of the earth,
> The realm of things that can be grasped, you

Agree with nature on a
Pact of solidarity: it is the right angle.
Standing up facing the sea, vertically
On your legs.[60]

The right angle is the human being and is a great cosmic sign.

"The horizontal limit of liquid capacity."[61]

The right angle is the sign of life.

When I lost my father, Le Corbusier wrote me a letter on 19 May 1960 in which he said:

"Death is the exit door for each one of us. I do not know why we want to make it awful. It is the horizontal of the vertical: complementary and natural."

It was necessary that he reached that last point, too, and drew his last right angle in space. On 27 August 1965, by the Mediterranean, Le Corbusier stood up. Upright, he went down the shore. Perhaps he picked one last pebble to feel its shape, polished by time, with his hand, between his fingers, against his palm. Upright, vertically, he went into the sea. Then he lay down at sea, horizontally, to die.

French architect André Wogenscky (1916–2004) worked at Le Corbusier's legendary Rue de Sèvres studio for twenty years (1936–56), where he eventually became the main associate. With Le Corbusier, he supervised the design and construction of such epoch-making buildings as the various *Unités d'Habitation* (Marseilles, Nantes, Berlin, Briey-en-Fôret, and Firminy). After leaving Le Corbusier, with whom he collaborated and maintained a friendship until the master's death in 1965, Wogenscky established an independent practice.

Starting with his own residence in Saint-Rémy-les-Chevreuse (1950–52), and continuing with the School of Medicine of the Necker Hospital in Paris (1963–65), the Maison de la Culture in Grenoble (1965–67), the Préfecture and Court House des Hauts-de-Seine in Nanterre (1965–72), the Beirut University master plan in Lebanon (1967–76), and the Takarazuka University of Arts and Design in Japan (1981–87), Wogenscky's built works effectively adapted and extended the Rue de Sèvres postwar vocabulary and humanist approach into the 1970s and 1980s to produce what he liked to call an "active architecture." Wogenscky installed his office in Le Corbusier's former apartment in Paris from 1973 until 1991, when he retired.

A member of Ascoral, UAM, Atbat, and CIAM, Wogenscky was a privileged witness to postwar architectural developments. As the director of the Fondation Le Corbusier (1971–82), he also contributed to the preservation of Le Corbusier's legacy. In 1987, as part of the centenary of Le Corbusier's birth, he published *Les mains de Le Corbusier,* his book on the Swiss-French master. The MIT Press is now pleased to present the English version.

NOTES

1 Le Corbusier, *Poème de l'angle droit* (Paris: Teriade, 1955).

2 Ibid.

3 Letter from Le Corbusier to Charles L'Eplattenier, dated 25 November 1908.

4 Ibid.

5 Ibid.

6 Letter from Le Corbusier to his team at 35 rue de Sèvres written in Simla on 6 November 1951.

7 Cited in an exhibition on "the city" at the RER station Etoile in Paris on opening day (20 February 1970).

8 *Le Corbusier* (Paris: Musée National d'Art Moderne, 1953).

9 Carlos Castaneda, *Le don de l'Aigle* (Paris: Gallimard, 1982), the French translation of Castaneda's *Eagles Gift*.

10 Le Corbusier, *Tapisseries de Le Corbusier* (Geneva and Paris: Musée d'Art et d'Histoire de Genève and Musée des Arts Décoratifs de Paris, 1975).

11 Le Corbusier, *Poème de l'angle droit.*

12 Le Corbusier, *Vers une architecture* (Paris: G. Crès, 1924).

13 Father Couturier's words are quoted from the author's memory.

14 Michel de Montaigne, *Essais* (book 1, chapter 26).

15 Ibid.

16 Rainer Maria Rilke, *The Sonnets to Orpheus* (2:5).

17 Le Corbusier, *Poème de l'angle droit.*

18 Montaigne, "Apologie de Raimond Sebond," *Essais* (book 2, chapter 12).

19 Rainer Maria Rilke, "Seventh Duino Elegy."

20 From a letter to Charles L'Eplattenier from Le Corbusier, dated 25 November 1908.

21 African saying the author heard on the radio.

22 *Le Corbusier.*

23 Le Corbusier, *Tapisseries de Le Corbusier.*

24 From a recorded interview included in Jacques Barsac's film *Le Corbusier* (produced by Service Ciné Technique, 1987).

25 *Le Corbusier.*

26 *Le Corbusier: Textes et dessins pour Ronchamp* (Geneva: Forces Vives, 1965).

27 Le Corbusier as quoted by Jean Petit in *Le Corbusier lui-même* (Geneva: Forces Vives, 1965).

28 Montaigne, *Essais* (book 2, chapter 1).

29 Le Corbusier, *Poème de l'angle droit.*

30 Ibid.

31 On the principles of the *Unité d'Habitation* and the Radiant City, see the author's preface to the first volume of Le Corbusier's complete drawings, devoted to the *Unité* at Marseilles (New York and Paris: Garland Publishing and Fondation Le Corbusier, 1983).

32 Letter by Le Corbusier dated 10 June 1931 published in Alberto Sartoris's *Gli elementi dell'architettura funzionale* (Milan, 1931), cited by Danièle Pauly in *Ronchamp: Lecture d'une architecture* (Paris: Ophrys, 1980).

33 From a lecture given by Frank Lloyd Wright at Princeton University in 1930, cited by Michel Ragon in *Histoire mondiale de l'architecture et de l'urbanisme moderne* (Tournai: Casterman, 1972), vol. 2.

34 This paragraph is taken from the author's preface to Russell Walden's edited book *The Open Hand: Essays on Le Corbusier* (Cambridge, Mass.: MIT Press, 1977).

35 Le Corbusier, *Quand les cathédrales étaient blanches* (Paris: Plon, 1937), written in 1934.

36 Ibid.

37 This paragraph is taken from the author's preface to Walden's *The Open Hand.*

38 Le Corbusier, *Quand les cathédrales étaient blanches.*

39 *Le Corbusier.*

40 Le Corbusier, "Les tendances de l'architecture rationaliste en relation avec la peinture et la sculpture," lecture given in Rome in 1936, published in *L'architecture vivante* (Paris: 1936), 7th series, and cited in Pauly's *Ronchamp.*

41 A quote from Lao-tzu found in an architecture magazine.

42 Le Corbusier, *Poème de l'angle droit.*

43 Antoine de Saint-Exupéry, as quoted in Robert Auzelle, "Propos d'un architecte," *Cahiers de l'Académie d'Architecture 1* (1981).

44 A slightly modified version of this text on light was published in the catalogue of the exhibition "Le Corbusier et la Méditerranée" (Marseilles: Musées de Marseille and Editions Paranthèses, June–September 1987).

45 Le Corbusier, *Le Modulor* (Paris: Editions de l'Architecture d'Aujourd'hui, 1950).

46 Ibid.

47 Le Corbusier, as quoted in Pauly's *Ronchamp*. The original quote is taken from a special issue of *L'architecture d'aujourd'hui* (April 1948) dedicated to Le Corbusier.

48 Le Corbusier, *Le Modulor*.

49 J. M. G. Le Clezio, *Haï* (Geneva: Skira, 1971).

50 From a lecture given by Le Corbusier in Venice in 1952, quoted by Pauly in *Ronchamp*.

51 Le Corbusier, *Poème de l'angle droit*.

52 Madame de Sévigné in a letter dated 7 June 1675 to Madame de Grignan.

53 Castaneda, *Le don de l'Aigle*.

54 Quoted by Dan Haulica during the symposium "L'Art dans la cité" (Prague, May 1987).

55 From a handwritten note by Le Corbusier dated 28 August 1955.

56 Ibid.

57 From a conversation with Le Corbusier recorded in the monastery of La Tourette and published by *L'architecture d'aujourd'hui* (June–July 1961).

58 Le Corbusier, "L'espace indicible," quoted in his *Modulor*.

59 From an article by André Kuenzi published in *La Gazette de Lausanne* (4–5 September 1965).

60 Le Corbusier, *Poème de l'angle droit*.

61 Ibid.

CAPTIONS OF IMAGES

BACK COVER PHOTO:

André Wogenscky, 2002. Photographer unknown. Courtesy of Archives André Wogenscky, Paris.